A SILENT SOLILOQUY

A JOURNEY WITHIN

SIDDHARTHA PAPPALA

Made with ♥ on the Notion Press Platform
www.notionpress.com

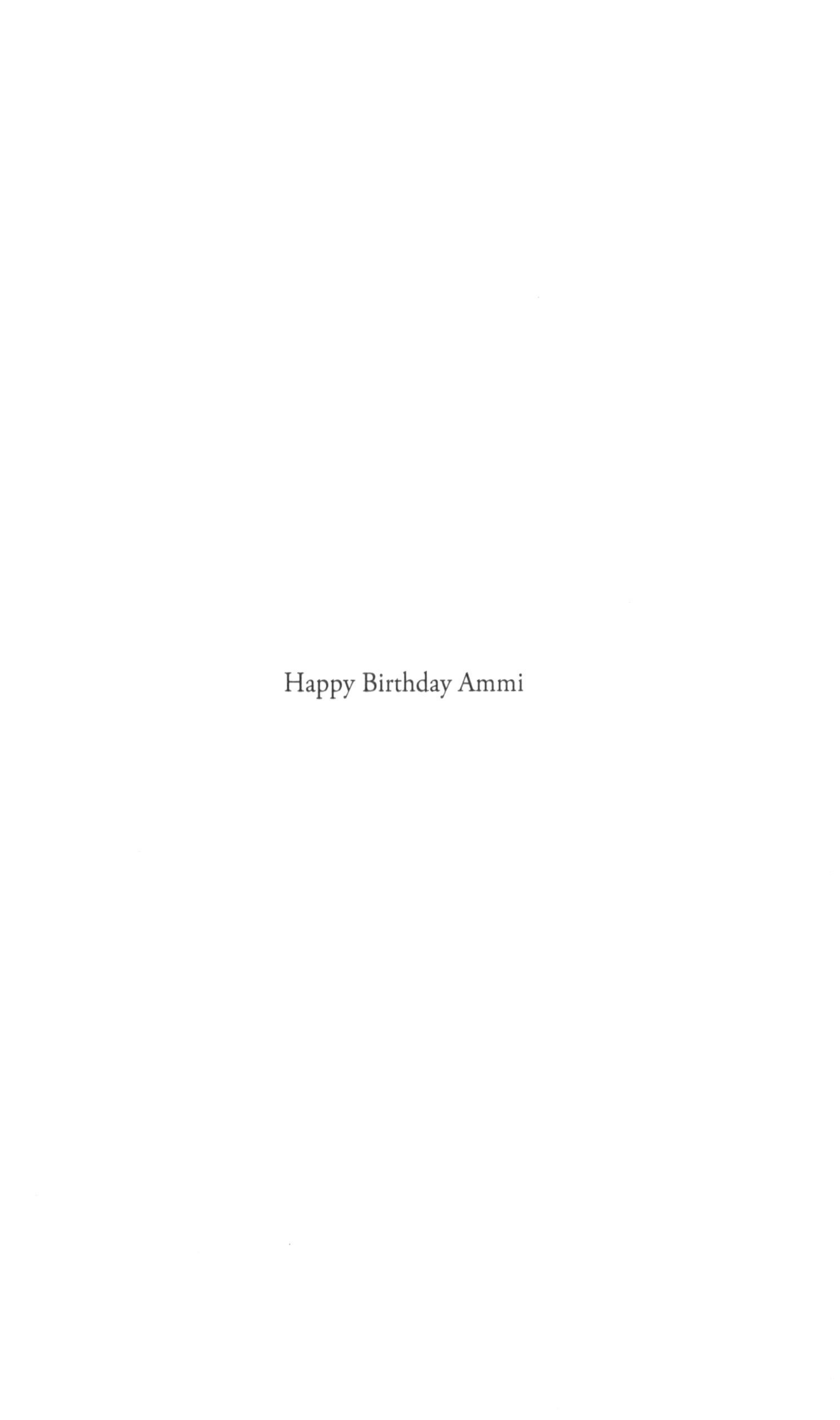

Happy Birthday Ammi

To

Mom & Dad

నా రాజు రావణుడు,

నా మాట వింటావా?

RAVANA IS MY KING,

WILL YOU LISTEN TO MY WORDS?

मेरा राजा रावण है,

क्या तुम मेरी बात सुनोगे?

Preface

When I first began this journey of writing, I did not set out to create a collection of poetry. For years, I've been scribbling lines in my notes—sometimes a complete poem, sometimes just a sentence, and in some instances, merely a word. It's only when Sruthi, my wife, started to push me to pen it down into a book, whether it was one or ten poems, that I found the courage to stitch it all together.

You see the irony—it's a battle of my own soliloquy. It then started as a need to express the unspoken, to capture the fleeting thoughts that swirled within my mind.

A Silent Soliloquy: A Journey Within is the culmination of that expression, a reflection of the inner dialogue that has accompanied me throughout my life.

I suggest you pick up this book only when you can relate to the true meaning of introspection and the dark reality that often accompanies it.

This isn't a book of joy, but rather one of pain, helplessness, and despair —emotions born from the struggles of the inner self and the external world.

In the pages that follow, you will find a blend of raw emotion and contemplative thought—a dance between light and shadow, hope and despair, love and loss.

My words are not just my own; they are echoes of a shared human experience, a testament to the silent battles we all face.

This book is not just a collection of poems; it is a journey—one that I invite you to take with me. Whether you find solace, inspiration, or even discomfort within these lines, I hope that they resonate with you in some way. For in the end, A Silent Soliloquy is about more than just my voice; it is about finding the courage to listen to your own.

Welcome to this journey within.

May it bring you closer to your own silent soliloquy.

Acknowledgement

When I sat down to write this part of the book, I was overwhelmed with emotion as I reflected on the countless individuals who have touched my life.

Each one, in their own way, has played a crucial role in shaping who I am today and in guiding my creative journey. To all of you, I extend my deepest gratitude.

"If you're reading this page and know me personally, it means you've touched my life and inspired me in ways that contributed to the creation of this book."

Contents

Preface   9

Acknowledgement   11

1. Who am I to judge your worth ?   16

2. A reason to hold on !!   18

3. Others' Faults   20

4. The 8th Mile   22

5. It's just a pause!!   26

6. A Sonnet to Reflect Myself   28

7. I Wish I Sleep in the Sea   30

8. The Path I Took   34

9. The COVID-19 Interlude   36

10. Self-Salted Scars   40

11. Eerie Echoes   46

12. Cards of Fate and Irony   50

13. A Night in the Bar with Jeeves and Wodehouse   54

14. Designed World of Consistency   60

15. The Genie and The Copper Clay Pot   64

16. Echoes of Nothingness   70

17. Embers in the Dark   74

18. Beneath the Surface   78

19. Where I Go: A Villanelle   84

20. The Endless Party   86

21. The Child in Me   90

22. I've debts to repay   92

23. Memory, You cruel beast   96

24. The Weight of Watching   100

25. A Lonely Peasant   104

15

•••

1. Who am I to judge your worth ?

I saw a man sleeping on a footpath,
As rain poured down relentlessly,
He shielded himself with a broken umbrella,
Discarded by someone, a token of their apathy.

Beside him stood a grand showroom,
Air-conditioned and empty,
No customers to grace its halls,
A stark contrast, a silent elegy.

We often question our difficult lives,
Why promotions elude, why trips are rare,
But seldom do we pause to appreciate,
The blessings we have, the love and care.

Should we compare with those who have more,
And feel disheartened by what we lack?
Or look at those with less than us,
And find joy in what we stack?

If you ask me, I'd say compare with none,
Appreciate what we hold so dear,
Help someone whenever we can,
And feel blessed to share and cheer.

Life is not a race of wealth,
But a journey of the heart,
To cherish, to give, to love,
That's where true riches start.

2. A reason to hold on !!

When fear claims your conscience's throne,
When dust corrodes your soul's core,
When silence drowns your heartfelt moan,
When solitude is your only door,

When darkness smothers your bright dreams,
When time plays foul with your destiny,
When blame tarnishes your innocence,
When 'guilt for nothing' resides in you,

Forget the fleeting, the fearful fight
Not shared moments, shining bright
Dismiss their pride, embrace their art,
Not their deeds, but love's warm start.

Disregard the doubt, dispel the haze,
Not their dread, but grateful days.
Smile and say, "I still need you!"
For in their absence, you're lost in blue.

Release the anger, let it fade,
Not the memories you once made.
Cast aside the heavy wrongs,
But keep their laughter, their sweetest songs.

Hold their kindness, not their fear,
Not the silence, but words sincere.
Through all the pain, don't be withdrawn,
For love remains, **a reason to hold on**.

3. Others' Faults

...It isn't the flesh, but the meat we eat...
...That ego in him...
...And that selfish her...
...Those brutal them...
...And the innocent us...

...Your jealous green words...
...And gossiping chats...
...My selfless soul...
...The judgments of the world...

...Their corner smiles...
...And the longing looks...
...My worn-out clothes...
...And your torn-out jeans...

...My fragile broken heart...
...And your drunken twists...
...My buried truths...
...And your sinful thoughts...

...My silent screams...
...And your fading dreams...
...My hidden tears...
...And your meaningless fears...

...It's always you...
...For the question 'who?'
... And if you ask me too...
... I'll say it's you, just as true....

4. The 8th Mile

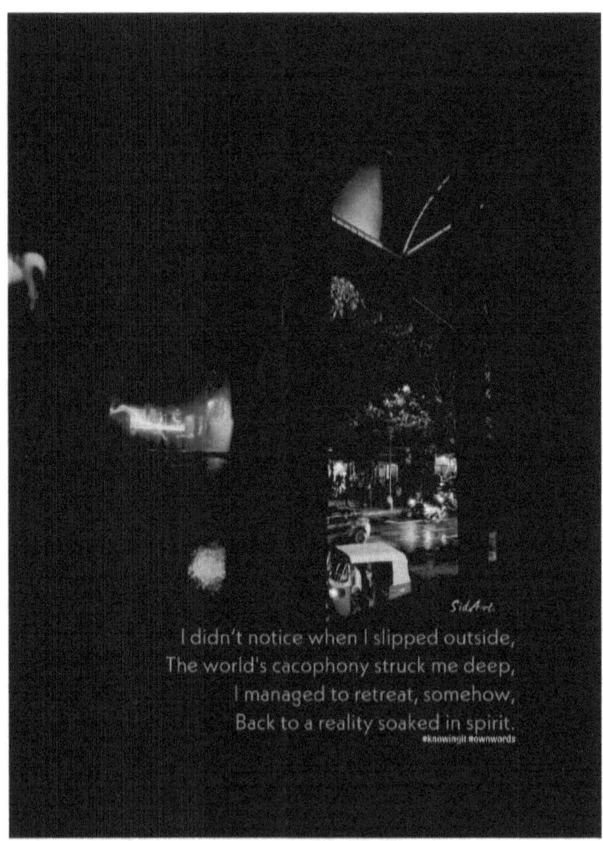

I ran to the eighth mile and saw a stone,
Inscribed with "Ninth mile is a mile beyond."
The paths were smooth, the ways were bright,
A dreamland waiting, just in sight.

But then I saw what I had missed,
A beautiful beast, fierce and unkissed.
Stopped at the third mile, faith in decay,
Worshipping a stone in a fervent display.

Her prayers turned the stone divine,
She wished my journey to be fine,
No hurdles, smooth, and swift to glide,
To reach the eighth mile, then by her side.

Yet at the eighth, the ninth did lie,
My success's end moved further high,
And I saw there's no final race,
No finish line, no stopping place.

A dark realization dawned on me,
The true success I could now see,
Was not the miles I left behind,
But her love, pure and kind.

I turned around, my path reversed,
Toward the love I always cherished,
Equal, strong, and selflessly,
She wished for my success to be.

Her strength and love, so clear and bright,
Guided me back through the night,
And back to her, I found my way,
In her arms, I wished to stay.

I find more joy in her embrace,
Than dreamlands in a distant space,
For in her love, I see my home,
No need to wander, no need to roam.

5. It's just a pause!!

I walked along the sides of the rail track,
Neither lost, nor wishing for a thwack.
I just walked, without knowing why,
As speeding trains kept rushing by.

No questions haunt me, none to chase,
No answers hidden, none to trace.
My life's no blaze of problems dire,
Yet I wander these rails, a soul on hire.

Perhaps it's just a pause, a brief reprieve,
A break in the bustle, a moment to believe.
Not my doing, nor another's scheme,
It simply happened, like a fleeting dream.

With a song humming softly in my mind,
An old refrain, its lyrics hard to find.
It gave me purpose, a quest to start,
But the path stayed hidden, deep in my heart.

The rails beneath hummed the same song,
A rhythm of life, neither right nor wrong.
With every step, I feel less bound,
Yet tethered to earth, not lost, not found.

I left the tracks and the forgotten song,
Looked to the sky, where night had drawn.
It's not your fault, there's nothing wrong,
Just a pause that ends with the break of dawn.

6. A Sonnet to Reflect Myself

When I'm not myself, the world looks strange and bright,
The reasons seem amusing, not profound,
The problems lose their depth, my thoughts take flight,
In widened vistas, dreams are newly found.

The fears of childhood fade, I'm filled with cheer,
A hopeful spirit rises up in me,
But should I seek to live this way, so clear,
Or find the means to always just be free?

Is this illusion better than the truth,
Where I am bound by struggles deep and real?
In fleeting moments, echoing my youth,
A happiness that's almost surreal.

A fragile balance, between light and dark,
Where shadows dance and hopes ignite the spark.
In this uncertain world, where truths unfold,
I seek a path, where stories will be told.

In fleeting moments, when the world stands still,
A quiet peace, a calm that I fulfill.
Yet, in the chaos, where doubts and fears reside,
I search for answers, where truth is tried.

Perhaps the truth lies in finding peace,
In both the dream and the reality's release.
So should I chase this altered state of mind,
Or seek the real, my true self, undefined?

7. I Wish I Sleep in the Sea

I sleep in the sea,
Cold and warm,
Deep and calm,
Just myself around me,

Thoughts sinking to the depths,
Hearing the silence of the oceans,
Feeling the deepest emotions,
I want to sleep in the sea.

I feel the moon, soft and light,
Stars flicker in the still of night,
Cradled by waves, gentle and free,
I feel free, seeing my fears flee .

I drift in depths where secrets lie,
The ocean's song, a soothing sigh,
Drifting slowly, fears released,
In the quiet, finding peace.

I hear currents whisper ancient tales,
Of sunken ships and hidden whales,
Weightless, floating, dreams unfold,
In the sea's depths, stories told.

I yearn for the depths, where secrets hide,
A tranquil haven, where I reside.
The ocean's touch, a soothing balm,
Calming my soul, easing the storm.

I drift and dream, where mermaids play,
In watery realms, day after day.
A peaceful haven, where I wish I've grown,
A world of wonders, now my own.

I breathe with the ocean's ebb and flow,
In the ocean's arms, I know,
A world apart, serene and wide,
Where I can simply be, inside.

I sleep in the sea so deep,
Where the heart can softly weep.
In this liquid world, I find,
I find rest, a quiet mind.

All this be my wishful plea,
The sea will heal and shelter me.
Take my fears and set them free,
I wish I could sleep in the sea.

8. The Path I Took

Why care to stop and listen to my story,
Why bother to hear a tale of less glory?
But if you have a minute and hear me out,
This is the path that I took, without a doubt.

Twists and turns, a path that's meant for me,
Thoughts unshared, words no one could see.
Buffers and blessings, both in disguise,
Challenges and joys, every day is a surprise.

To a precious few, I was their gentle tide,
The weight of their trust, only they decide.
To a handful of many, I was a passing sight,
Unseen and unheard, hidden from the light.

I ditched, I danced, times were intricate,
At moments, I struggled to navigate.
I lied, I loved, souls forever moved apart,
Kindness and cruelty, shared from the same heart.

What I've realized is few lives we see up close,
A hundred more from a distance as life flows.
Thousands more we glimpse from far away,
But the full story of anyone, we can't convey.

Now that you've heard and know my chronicle,
You might feel it's not quite ideological.
If I heard yours, you too might not be a hero,
But it's our lives, and we must say, "Te quiero."

9. The COVID-19 Interlude

In twenty-twenty, a year of dread,
The world stood still, as if struck dead.
The roaring twenties, a decade of speed,
Came to a halt, a sudden decreed.

A young woman, Sasha, sat at her window,
Watching the world outside, a silent show.
The bustling streets, now eerily still,
A surreal scene, a chilling thrill.

We were racing through days, our pace so swift,
Then suddenly, we found a rift.
A pause, a halt, a moment's breath,
All around us, silence, like death.

No longer running, just standing still,
Breathing deeply, time to fill.
We looked back at lives we led,
Reflecting on the paths we once tread.

No more questions chasing dreams,
No more answers bursting at seams.
Life's problems took a gentler tone,
In this quiet, we found our own.

Talking, sharing, lives laid bare,
Stories exchanged with loving care.
Hours and days lost their might,
Living simply, felt so right.

Sasha watched the city sleep,
A silent world, so peaceful, deep.
The hustle and bustle, now laid to rest,
A chance to reflect, to be our best.

In love with self, with others too,
Worrying about what next to do.
Helping others, feeling plight,
Saluting workers in their fight.

Earphones off, the world we heard,
Songs of birds and cries absurd.
Dogs on streets, hunger and need,
Dolphins came, a wondrous deed.

Creepers reached with love to show,
Flowers bloomed, their dance did glow.
From skyscraper tops, we saw the sky,
Pink and green, caught by the eye.

Ganges pure, holy stream,
Nature's cleanse, a sacred dream.
Egos faded, time well spent,
With partners dear, in content.

Books were dusted, hobbies found,
Stories told with joy profound.
Children laughed at tales we spun,
Old and young, together as one.

A race no more, a life to live,
To kith and kin, our time we give.
Words of warmth, no need for gold,
Happiness that can't be sold.

For a moment, a dream it seemed,
But it was real, this life redeemed.
As time moved on, normal returned,
Frozen moments, lessons learned.

We found solace in nature's grace,
The birdsong filled the empty space.
A newfound appreciation for the green,
A connection to the world unseen.

And so we set an example bright,
For Gen-Alpha, future's light.
Remember this, when times are tough,
Life's not a race, living's enough.

10. Self-Salted Scars

If in the end, In the doom,

Not of the world, but of you and me,

What I think, what I do,
It holds weight and is true.
What you say, what you convey,
Doesn't truly have any sway.

Don't keep hope, I say to you,
But I don't believe in what you hear too,
In whom you thought I am,
I might be even your biggest scam.

You didn't care who was hurt,
I didn't know who felt for me.
All you know is all I did,
And all I did is all you wanted to get rid.

I wish I could ask for your forgiveness,
But why did you trust? It isn't your blitheness.
If I'm to be blamed, so are you,
You gave me a chance, I took you into a trance.

Gone are the times to question who took a chance,
Or who had a choice in this eternal dance.
For now, you know I'm not to trust,
Gone are the times when thoughts adjust.

Now I'm all alone, and so are you.
One to the right, and one to pursue.
One for the right and one for the left,
You and me, all alone, bereft.

I feel suffocated and you feel detested,
Suffocated by trust, and kindness invested.
Because you still feel I want you,
But that's not true, through and through.

You feel detested because of me,
Not realizing it was because of thee.
If it wasn't your will to turn around,
And go back to days when love was found.

How could you still not shatter,
With all that hate and blame on a platter?
If I were you, I would die,
Or choose an immortal life to cry.

You said, "Those who come to me, I suck them all,
And squeeze through the heart's narrow hall."
How dare you say when you were the one
Who taught me to be as I've become?

Others say I did wrongs and live along,
But crazy are those who don't know my song.
My hurt is deep, and fate was grim,
But I chose paths that made me dim.

Where do you get strength, for you are the reason
To stand strong and blame in season?
What do you do when you close your eyes?
Don't truths hit you with your lies?

If you think I'm coming after my doom,
Remember you've nothing for my room.
My actions and words aren't different from yours.
If you offer, it's just foolish chores.

We both tread the same life's path,
One chose right, one felt wrath.
I wish I taught some love's part,
That shows how to feel, not be apart.

But now you ask what I'd change,
Given a chance, I'd choose the same range.
But here's the truth you fail to see,
The one I blame, it's really me.
For in this battle of heart and mind,
It's my own self I often find.

Now, I'm all alone, and so are you,
For both sides of me, what can I do?
One side is right, the other out of line,
Both parts of me, in conflict confined.

• • •

11. Eerie Echoes

Why do I witness eerie beings,
for their souls were said to rest in peace,
Why do I hear moaning whispers,
for I know their lips were stuck in freeze?

Why do I speak to holy ghosts,
as if there are no people around,
Why do I fear becoming them,
though the truth lies deep in the ground?

Dark rooms and creepy places,
are these the places where I belong,
Faded faces and shattered glass,
why is everyone stuck with the same old song?
Insane stories of endless worries,
how long they preach these haunting glories,
Am I tired of how the world has turned?

And I wonder why ... why do I...

Silent cries in empty halls,
don't you hear your echoes in shadowed walls,
Twisted paths and broken dreams,
you are lost in a maze of silent screams,
Lingering ghosts of forgotten fears,
will haunt you through the endless years,
Why don't your fragile bones stir to life,

And I wonder why ... why do I...

Your souls were long lost in the midnight air,
your secrets hidden in a lifeless stare,
Phantom hands that reach and grasp,
pulling you into your haunted past,
Dread spectres of regret and sorrow,
offering no hope for tomorrow,
Why don't your fogged brain discern these spectral ties,

And I wonder why ... why do I...

Your hopes are shattered in this fractured sky,
lingering around an eaten moon that seems to sigh,
It's time for you to walk on land,
else even your manes will not hold your hand,
Time is fading and memories are distorting,
Why don't your hollow self-seek light and rise in joy,

And I wonder why ... why do I...

12. Cards of Fate and Irony

I'm a soothsayer, a tarot reader in distant lands,
What I say may come true, though it's not what I planned.
The cards stay the same, but my tales about you do vary,
Depending on whether I'm sober or feeling quite merry.

Sometimes when I'm alone, I dare to read my fate,
And every time I do, things just twist and rotate.
Once I saw I'd win the lottery, but ended up with a cat,
Another time, I predicted fame, but got chased by a rat.

But don't mess with me; I can draw a card for you,
And don't be afraid; many words will bless you too.
The cartoons on my deck are funny to me,
But scary to those who trust what they see.

A seer once said I'd foretell others' ways,
I heeded his words, lost in a prophetic haze.
Had I forged my own path, not followed his lore,
Maybe I'd be rich, not guessing at this store.

Perhaps a chef, creating fine cuisine,
Instead of telling fortunes, that might have been.
But here I am, with a shining crystal ball,
Wondering if I could've had it all.

It's funny when I read for others, what I see,
Their actions don't match the dreams they wish to be.
Every time I draw a card, I see a spark of belief,
And they trust every word, though I share their disbelief.

Times will be good if you accept the unknown,
Things will be fine, if you set the right tone,
Thoughts will waver, they wander and unravel,
You have the choice, you're the master of your marvel.

Wish for your own peace, feel it every day,
Wish for others' joy, you too will find a brighter way.
Focus on your fears, they will manifest,
Think only of loss, and you'll never feel blessed.

Life is a circle, it always comes back around,
Phases pass, joyous and grim, each moment crowned.
What was once a feast might now be just a bite,
What was once a mess might now be a delight.

Known far and wide, a tarot reader's stride,
And every time I draw a card, they place their fate inside.
Why fear the future, letting worry take control,
When today is yours to cherish and nurture your soul.

13. A Night in the Bar with Jeeves and Wodehouse

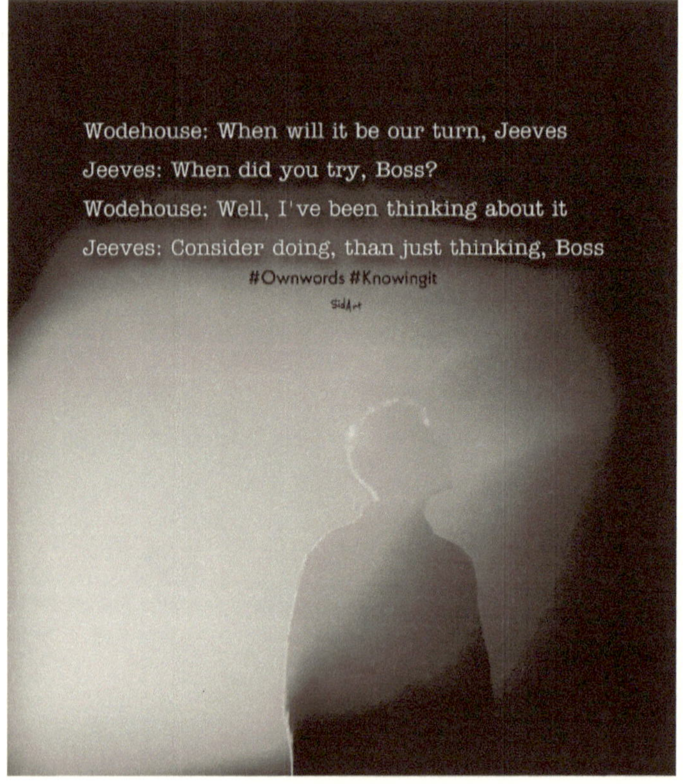

In a dim-lit bar, where shadows play,
Sat Jeeves and Wodehouse, come what may.
Glasses clinked with a gentle sway,
Both high, lost in a wordless fray.

Wodehouse spoke first, with a cryptic tone,
With a hearty cheer and of a mind's unknown.
In nonsensical, drunken sight.
Each word a puzzle, each phrase a flight,

"The moon's a mirror, shattered and sown,
He mused, yet sense remained unshown.
"Ah, the stars, they're but a chandelier!"
His mind adrift, with thoughts unclear,
Reality, a far-off sphere.

Jeeves began with a slur and a grin,
"Let's get this straight sir, where shall we begin?
I hate you to the core, it's uncouth.
This thing inside, it can't stay mute."

"Sir, So many fiascos have brought me here,
From trousers torn to flatulent cheer.
Life's cruel pranks, a bitter jest,
Leaving my patience sorely pressed."

"Sir, High school failed to teach the art,
Of guarding secrets, playing smart.
Church said to forgive, pray for peace,
Yet here we are; our troubles never cease."

"Even you, sir, you've been misled,
By life's tough rules, and tears unshed.
We hang like bats, our faces pale,
In this world, where dreams derail."

"Oh these ad commercials sir, shining bright,
Do you think they're really right?
Illusions sell, dreams portrayed,
Honesty lost, often betrayed."

"Fake tans, fake smiles, all for show,
Reality twisted, we all know.
Sir, our Darling neighbour, wrinkled and old,
She's more real, frankly, more bold."

"So let's toast to what we see,
Fake or real, let it be.
Cheers to life, sir; cheers to fate,
In this bar, it's never late."

"But, Sir, no quick fix makes one sleek,
A movie won't alter the strong or weak.
Egos remain; they're hard to shake,
We're not sleeping beauties, for heaven's sake."

"Sir, life's a game, a twisted ride,
Here we sit, nowhere to hide.
Sharing nonsense, truths so raw,
In this dim-lit, hazy draw."

"Economy, sir, tamed yet wild,
While hunger prowls, it is never mild
Pie in the sky, hopes so vain,
We spin the same yarns; we are all the same."

"Sir, Injustice rules and promises faint,
I pay my dues, yet I've had complaints.
Streetlights dead, taxes high,
Modern kings, they lie and lie."

"Politicians, promises, nothing they deliver,
Sir, our spirits sink while woes linger.
What an age, what a disgrace!
Long for kings, history's embrace."

"I studied history, sir; names I recall,
Kings and queens, the great and the small,
 Doubt me, sir? I'll prove my worth,
Alexander's might, Cleopatra's mirth."

"Akbar and Birbal, friends like us,
Dined and drank without a fuss.
Empty jugs, where's our beer, dear Wooster?
Fill them up, old chap, make us cheer!"

"While Jeeves ranted, words in a whirl,
Not caring if Wodehouse heard at all.
Lost in wine, in his own sweet swirl,
Wodehouse murmured to his love, enthralled."

As Jeeves ranted on, with thoughts in a whirl,
Wodehouse lifted his glass, lost in a swirl.
"Darling, I love you," he whispered to his wine,
Lost in bubbles, their light divine.

The bar around them faded to grey,
As time inched forward, thoughts decayed.
No heed to sense, in their minds' display,
Just cryptic words in a stoned array.

And so they drank till the night was a blur,
Two minds unwound as dawn began to stir.
Wodehouse mumbled, "What now, what's the spur?"
"Just as you say, there is a letter on the tray, sir."

14. Designed World of Consistency

To those days of mental slavery and those chains that bound,
To moments where agony was celebrated, bitterly profound,
I abandon this world designed for consistency,
And choose to suffer in happiness, unquenched by complacency.

I wandered among the faceless men, lost in their haze,
With half-hearted wits, indifferent to life's maze.
Noble duties bore them, indulgence leave their feet cold,
So I left their company, even at my peak, bold and untold.

I ask these questions, now relentless ,clear and strong
Why did I linger in spaces where I don't belong ?
Your sinking ship isn't mine to save,
Why did it take so long to find the courage to be brave?

What I demand of you is hard to bear,
What I expect of myself is beyond compare.
Should I laugh at your plight or try to teach?
Either way, I see you fall, forever out of reach.

You dreamed of glory, yet your questions are dry
Spineless actions reveal the hollow in your cry.
Sit now, for I won't be a martyr for your lost cause,
I refuse to point fingers when I know the flaws.

You follow orders from voices long gone,
Words that may have once been wise, now withdrawn
I can't speak their language, but my truth remains,
And I won't follow a path where frustration reigns.

You wait, you seek, you crave their approval,
But never question why you're bound to their removal.
You treat, you mistreat, in fear of what they say,
But blindly follow a norm that's lost its way.

You're lucky in your ignorance, wrapped in a lie,
But I choose the pain of truth, and in that, I fly.
To question, to challenge, to break from the mould,
For in my suffering, my spirit is bold.

15. The Genie and The Copper Clay Pot

In the depths of time, where shadows rest,
A copper clay pot held a soul, blessed.
For years it stayed, in silence, in peace,
Its world complete, with no need for release.

But one fateful day, with a curious hand,
Someone rubbed the copper clay pot, breaking the stand.
The Genie within, forced out with a sigh,
Flew into the world, under a vast sky.

They cheered, those hands, thinking it's free,
Believing the Genie would dance with glee.
But what they saw was not what it seemed,
For freedom to them was not the Genie's dream.

To the world outside, the pot was mere copper clay,
A vessel to hold, a place to stay.
But to the Genie, it wasn't mere , but much more,
There's a world in itself, rich in lore.

Within its walls, a paradise thrived,
A garden of dates, where the spirit survived.
An oasis of calm, a place so true,
Where the Genie found peace, life was new.

The world beyond was a sea so wide,
But to the Genie, it was a fearsome ride.
For the men who freed it, the world was bright,
But to the Genie, it was a distant fright.

They saw riches, gems, and golden fields,
They built their lives on what the earth yields.
But to the Genie, these things were vain,
For in its copper clay pot, it felt no pain.

The men wore masks, their true faces hidden,
Their true selves lost, their hearts forbidden.
They sought out places, unknown, unseen,
While the Genie longed for the familiar, the serene.

In their eyes, the world was grand,
A red apple orchard, a snowy land.
They marvelled at mountains, rivers wide,
But the Genie saw a mirage, a fleeting tide.

Why should it leave the copper clay pot it knew?
Why chase the world when its heart was true?
For them, the world was a place to roam,
But for the Genie, the copper clay pot was home.

They searched for treasures, far and wide,
But the Genie's treasure was locked inside.
They drew maps of lands so rare,
But the Genie's map led only to despair.

It questioned its path, its place, its role,
Should it wander like them, or stay whole?
Should it pretend to enjoy their endless chase,
Or return to its copper clay pot, its only safe place?

In the copper clay pot, it found a dream so sweet,
A life fulfilled, a joy complete.
Why seek diamonds in rivers deep,
When in the copper clay pot, it could peacefully sleep?

They painted pictures, delicate and fine,
But the Genie's art was of a different kind.
It saw the world through a different lens,
Where solitude and peace were its only friends.

Invisible to those who sought it out,
It flew back home, away from doubt.
Closed the lid, and turned to stay,
In the copper clay pot, it found its way.

Neither dead, nor lost in despair,
But living a life, beyond their glare.
In its world, both small and vast,
My Genie found a peace that would last.

The noble men of the world, they never knew,
The truth of what, the Genie went through.
For in their world of gold and might,
They missed the beauty of a simpler light.

The Genie lived on, in its pot of copper clay,
Invisible to all, day after day.
It found its joy, its endless bliss,
In the life it chose, a life like this.

16. Echoes of Nothingness

Ignore logic, plunge into the brink.
Words are thorns dipped in blood's ink.
Thoughts, ancient echoes, a haunting refrain,
Arms outstretched, in endless pain.

Days stretch on, a desolate expanse,
Paths muddy, shoes tracing a weary race,
Breasts and hearts, a tragic circumstance.
Black and white, a meaningless fray,
Life's a burden, a fading ray.

Embrace the soul, a futile quest,
Avoid the shadows, a haunting test.
Eyes reflect despair, a vacant stare,
Lips form lies, a poisoned snare.

Tears like rivers, a ceaseless flow,
Pain's a tempest, a mournful woe.
Hands that cradle, also can destroy,
A fleeting moment, a shadowed joy.

Time, a relentless, unforgiving tide,
Dreams, like ashes, scattered wide.
Words can wound, or offer a mend,
In silence, the soul's secrets transcend.

The world, a stage for shadows deep,
Through every twist, our sorrows seep.
Embrace the soul, a barren land,
A solitary soul, without a hand

A cosmic jest, a cruel design,
Existence, a meaningless line.
A phantom limb, a haunting trace,
Lost in the depths, a vacant space.

A hollow shell, a shattered heart,
Torn apart, right from the start.
A void, a chasm, an endless night,
Consuming all, with blinding light.

A whisper lost, a fading sound,
In nothingness, forever bound.
A cosmic dance, a futile play,
A meaningless existence, day by day.

An empty canvas, a barren land,
A soul adrift, without a hand.
A final curtain, a fading scene,
In endless darkness, lost from sight.

A nothingness, a void complete,
Where silence reigns, a solemn retreat.
A final chapter, a closing door,
In this existence, evermore.

A solitary soul, adrift in space,
A vacant stare, a lifeless face.
A silent scream, a cosmic plea,
For oblivion, eternally.

In shadows deep, I find my end,
Where meaning fades, and shadows blend.
A final breath, a whispered sigh,
As darkness claims me, I will die.

17. Embers in the Dark

The Weight of Existence :

The face I wear bears the weight of days,

Where delicate happenings bring heavy haze.

Dreams, like shattered glass, pierce my core,

Opportunities missed, forevermore.

I stand still, roots deep in the ground,

A world of consistency, where I'm bound.

Commonness finds a new role in dust,

Fate writes my destiny, in glorified disgust.

The Mockery of Self :
Finding meaning in this void I tread,
Mockery paints my face with a smile, unsaid.
Failed in light, failed in fame,
I find solace in accepting blame.
Invisible cloak, grace in my fall,
Succumbing to whispers that haunt and call.
Glistening grease before swans' might,
A life without bread, a long, dark night.
The world, a stage for swans of pristine white, While shadows
dance in the fading light.

The Smoke of Shame :
Shame surrounds me, a smoke so dense,
Suffocating life, with a passion immense.
Scared of love, both near and far,
I retreat into rust, beneath the scar.
In serenity's homicide, I taste the tears,
Of fear, mistrust, and dejection's spears.
The bridge to solace, a memory long gone,
Only the valleys of melancholy I've known.
Present tense drives fate to mould my despair,
A glorified puke on the hopes I once dared.

The Cold Reality :
You dream of glory, your actions frail,
Spineless deeds reveal your tale.
Sit now, for I refuse to fight,
Against your hollow, fading light.
You follow orders from voices old,
While I seek truths, yet untold.
I won't walk your path of despair,
For I've chosen to rise, aware.
In the depths of sorrow, joy takes flight,
A dance of contrasts, dark and light.

The Sculpted Self :
I've become a sculpture, hard and cold,
With wisdom born from grief, untold.
A rock, no use, but heavy with pain,
Hoping for clouds to bring down rain.
Fish in the sky, filling empty seas,
Carrying burdens to the edge with ease.
For in the end, all I've known,
Is a journey that leaves me alone.
To suffer in happiness, unquenched by ease,
In the suffering of unfulfilled dreams, I find peace.

Defiance in the Dark :

The face I wear mirrors the world's harsh hand,

A fragile vessel in shifting sand.

Dreams, like shattered glass, pierce my core,

Opportunities missed, forevermore.

My heart, a rusted cage, desires to sing,

But fear's cold grip, its voice won't bring.

Shame, a shroud that binds me tight,

Love's abundant grace, banished from sight.

The Ember of Hope :

Yet within the depths of brooding despair,

A flicker of defiance, a strength I can share.

Battles fought, though etched with defeat,

Sculpt wisdom that's bittersweet.

The path ahead, shrouded in endless night,

But I hold the ember, a beacon of light.

In the suffering of unquenched dreams,

I find my peace in life's extremes.

18. Beneath the Surface

Those silent dwellings in each life's deep core,

Lies a shadowed realm where you hear echoes softly roar.

With its passed phases , wishes turned cold,

Dreams were shattered, their fragments always told.

Alone, unheard, its solitary sound,

In this dark hermit space, we atone.

It was one of those misty nights, I walked,
Seeking peace from life's relentless clock.
A melody played, soft and light,
My phone, a mentor through the darkest night.
But a reminder broke the harmony's flow,
A picture of friendship from years ago.

A ghostly smile, as night's chill deepened slow,
Alone with shadows, where secrets grow.
Memories surfaced, like echoes of the past,
Things I repent , forever to last.
The empty path, a stage for solitude's art,
Each step, a chapter, a brand new start.

At pathway's end, a spectral form appeared,
A shadowed smile, where doubt and fear adhered.
A face divided, light and darkness blend,
Shared years, a tale without an end.
Searching for answers, a reason why,
Their hidden depths, a haunting cry.

Is there a darkness in me unknown?
A part of my own life, never shown?
Or have I been too blind to see,
A masked existence, haunting me?
A chilling doubt, a question's icy sting,
As night's cold fingers, doubts they bring.

In life's grand stage, a vibrant show
Some we know, some we only think we know.
We see the gleaming surface, a captivating art,
While shadows whisper, hidden from their hearts.
Indeed, a shadowed self in every great soul,
Its dark silent stories, a haunting grey role.

No masked pretence, no cunning art,
Just shadows hidden within the heart.
A silent prison, where fears reside,
A captive spirit, where hope can hide.
Before we seek to heal another's pain,
Must we first confront our own domain?

How often do we walk side by side,
With those whose secrets they carefully hide?
A smile, a nod, a shared glance or two,
But the real stories remain out of view.
Connected threads, yet worlds unknown,
Stories untold, a haunting tone.

What burdens do we carry in the dark?
Unseen weights that leave their mark.
We mask the pain, we hide the scars,
Wishing for solace in distant stars.
But in this silent, shadowed space,
We confront our fears face to face.

Do I see in others what I fail to see,
The hidden parts that also dwell in me?
A mirrored image, light and dark entwined,
Silent dreams, ambitions undefined.
In every face, a piece of mine,
In every story, a trace of time.

Life's a stage, a drama of light and shade,
In every scene, a climax is made.
To reveal, to hide, to speak, to stay,
In the twilight zone, we find our way.
But what we show is never all,
For shadows rise, and shadows fall

Am I a solitary wanderer, lost in thought,
What shadows linger, what secrets are caught?
What do I hide behind my smile?
What fears do I bury, mile after mile?
In seeking truth, a labyrinth I tread,
Will answers come, or doubts instead?

A silent cry from darkness' core,
Yearning freedom, forevermore.
A voiceless plea, unheard, unknown,
In shadowed battles, we stand alone.
We live with shadows, we learn to cope,
But still, we search for a thread of hope.

As I walk this path, under the moon's soft glow,
I realize there's so much I'll never know.
About myself, about those I meet,
About the secrets they choose to keep.
Yet, in this journey, a solace I find,
Acceptance's balm for the troubled mind.

19. Where I Go: A Villanelle

Where I go is a winding path of dust and despair,
Or is this the end of a fruitless affair?
Where I stand is where shadows linger and snare.

Where I stand is where kindred souls find their lair,
But does this connection, burdens or repair?
Where I go is Where dreams ignite, and passions flare.

Where I go is where human spirits chase phantasy's glare,
Isn't it just a cosmic snare?
Where this ends, this life, is beyond compare.

Where I stand is a speck in the cosmic sea,
Will purpose ever reveal itself to me?
Where I go , this destiny, can it set me free?

Where I go, this destiny, an inevitable decree,
Does freedom truly exist, can't you see?
Where this ends, this life, is a mystery.

I'm no puppet to dance to fate's cruel plea,
Can I break free before I cease to be?
Where I stand is where dreams dissolve like a spree.

A soul adrift, a spirit longing to be,
Lost in a labyrinth with no guarantee,
Where shadows creep, and darkness consumes me.
Where I go is where someone must have once been.

20. The Endless Party

Why can't life be a party so fine,
Where all doubts fade and joy aligns?
No hangovers to bear,
No guilt to ensnare,
Just laughter and joy on demand.

We played as kids, carefree and bright,

Our days were a party, a pure delight.

Now grown-ups we roam,

Searching for home,

That joy we once knew, shining so light.

A party with music so bright,

That plays through the day and the night.

No past to recall,

No future at all,

Just dancing in pure, endless light.

No bruises, no burns, a perfect scene,

No kicks, no worries, a peaceful dream.

A party that spins,

Forever begins,

A world of pure joy, serene.

But why keep this joy just for you?
Invite others in, make it true.
Share the laughter, spread the cheer,
A party for all, far and near,
A celebration where hearts renew.

When heavy thoughts begin to weigh,
Let's push them gently far away.
In this bright place,
Let's fill with grace,
Our hearts with joy, come what may.

With jingles that echo so clear,
And rhythms that ring in your ear.
No sorrow, no fears,
Just clinking of cheers,
In a world where fun's always near.

Random stuff makes it surreal,
Where nothing is quite what you feel.
A world to explore,
With surprises in store,
In a party that's perfectly ideal.

A party so perfect, a dream come true,
With gentle rain, a refreshing hue.
The gods would aspire,
To join this desire,
A heavenly bliss, forever new.

When the party ends and lights go dim,
It leaves a song, a lasting hymn.
A tune we'll sing,
Through life's every swing,
Keeping the joy alive within.

21. The Child in Me

The child in me, forever young, still yearns to play,
Holding dreams that never seem to sway.
Echoes of laughter, mingled with strife,

Caught in the middle of a double-edged life.
Hues of saffron and green blur in his sight,
In a world where battles are no longer bright.
Lines of faith cross with ease,
Dreaming of unity, of hearts at peace.

In riches and poverty, what do we find?
Not wealth but contentment eases his mind.

Madam and sir, mere titles in his jest,
Even in death, he's much better than the rest.

In shadows and power, lies often rise,
Slipping truth beneath their disguise.

Shallowness reigns where merit should climb,
The child in me, believes in the sublime.
In a dreamer's heart, wild and free,
Lies the true essence of glee.
Life's illusions, wealth pursued with zeal,

A fool's errand, a hollow deal.
Light shines not on the golden crown,
It's in kindness, where riches are found.
Victory is sought in the still of night,
Embracing the dark, where stars ignite.

22. I've debts to repay

I thrive in the heat of a mess,
While you flounder, your guts in distress.
You croak like a frog,
In a boiling smog,
And drown in your weakness, no less.

I've seen fires burn from inside,
Scars that no skin could ever hide.
You talk about pain?
You don't know the strain,
Of walking through hell while you cried.

There were times we stood side by side,
But you folded, you fled, you lied.
Dined with our foes,
Played both highs and lows,
And left me alone, bruised but defied.

You beg for a chance, to be spared,
But mercy from me? You're unprepared.
I hold your fate now,
I'll end it somehow,
But for now, your pathetic plea is aired.

It's not 'bout the weight of your fall,
Or the blood that will soon stain the wall.
It's the rhythm I choose,
How I'll make you lose—
Should I dance while I silence it all?

There's no "hope" in the pause that you see,
Just a countdown till you cease to be.
I've debts to repay,
For those who stayed grey,
And you? You'll learn what it means to face me.

I decide when you'll draw your last breath,
When your shadow's consumed by death.
No thoughts of remorse,
Just pure, brutal force—
And I'll smile while I script your last steps.

I am the master of this fight,
And your fate's locked in by tonight.
Crisis is my game,
I don't need your shame,
And you'll never escape from this plight.

23. Memory, You cruel beast

The memory I hold—

A blessing,

A curse.

Memory,
You make me suffer,
For all that's been lost,
Long gone, buried deep,
And yet, you whisper, *"Good old days."*

You make me repent,
For choices I made,
Back when they felt right,
Now, they feel like chains I forged myself.

Memory,
You cruel beast.
What's your game?
You let others live in peace,
The ones who never valued you—
They move on,
They forget,
While you drag me back,
Night after night,
To haunt me with ghosts of might-have-been,
That no longer exist.

Memory,
You cruel beast.
Why do you torment?
You fade for the common flock,
Those who suffer from the hands of others,
But you linger in the minds of the few,
Who bear the weight of the harm they caused.
You cling like a shadow that never tires,
A relentless echo that won't fade,
Reminding them of all they cannot escape.

Memory,
You cruel beast.
Why do you laugh?
You thrive in stories others tell,
In books others write,
In songs others sing,
Detached from the pain,
No scars on their hearts.
But you spit venom at those who lived it—
The ones who bled,
Who wrote the truth in their own blood,
At that moment, in real time.

Memory,
Why do you choose?
Why do you pick the few,
And fill them with endless weight,
While others walk free,
Their debts unpaid, forgotten?
Why do you stay with me,
Like a noose tightening each night,
When all I want is to let go?

Memory,
You cruel beast.

24. The Weight of Watching

I saw a lost couple,
Hands held tight,
Walking into the bar,
Disappearing from sight,
Their destinies untold, wrapped in the night.

Two bald men at the counter,
Debating their spot.
They talk, they argue,
But decide on naught,
Which table to sit at? Doesn't matter a lot.

A gang of friends all dressed in white,
A symbol of unity, yet something's not right.
Each orders different, their own delight,
Quiet rebellion in plain sight.

A gay couple next to me,
Admiring each other's beards, letting others see,
They laugh about their pubic hair,
Flipping cigarettes in the air,
Lost in a private, smoky sea.

In the corner, an office crowd,
Formal smiles, no words too loud.
But inside, they seem to lost a fight,
Each trapped in a solitary plight,
Waiting for the next forced mood to feel right.

Few sleeveless hip-hops, low-rise jeans,
Trying too hard to fit the scene.
One adjusts her plunging top,
The other lets her thoughts just drop,
Drowning in a rhythm no one's seen.

A man sits alone, his eyes on the floor,
Checking his phone, wishing for something more.
But the screen stays blank, nothing to say,
He scrolls, he sighs, then looks away,
A ghost of a man with no part to play.

A woman leans close to her wine, her whisper too soft,
Her laughter brittle, her drink held aloft.
She eyes the room, the faces she knows,
But her gaze drifts far, where no one goes,
Hiding the cracks in the smile she shows.

And here I am, sitting alone,
Sipping my Geist, flesh to bone.
Watching them all, hearing their minds,
Feeling their stories, but reading the signs—
Wondering, do I really stand on my own?

25. A Lonely Peasant

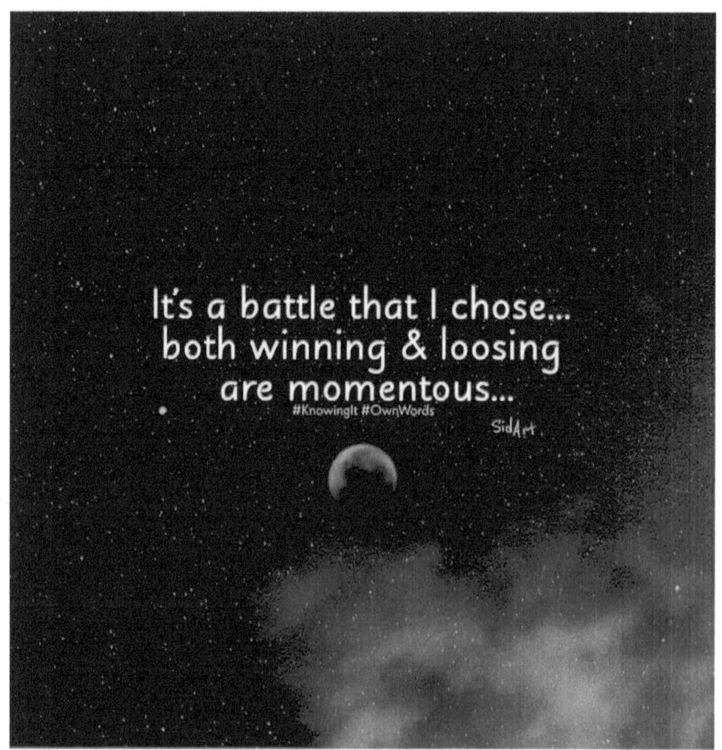

I am a lonely peasant,
Selling the fruits
That fell from the forbidden tree,
Amid the clamour of the common world,
To the laws and souls of the familiar earth.

I don't care to bargain,
I don't want them to haggle or plead,
Nor do I want them to pay a price
For the things that should be given freely.

I stand in the shadows, unseen by the rest,
Watching them haggle, desperate and stressed.
They fight for the scraps, the pieces I leave,
Blind to the truth that they've chosen to grieve.

I don't offer my wares to be praised or adored,
Nor do I care for the wealth they've stored.
The fruits I bear aren't for sale,
They're the remnants of a deeper tale.

They come with their coins and their empty greed,
But I can't sell what their souls truly need.
For what they crave, no price can define—
It's been rotting in silence, far beyond time.

I am a lonely peasant
With nothing to gain,
And everything lost to the hunger for pain.
Let them keep their gold, their bloodstained pay,
The fruits of the forbidden were never meant to stay.

I won't haggle or plead,
Let them keep their gold,
For what I hold is mine alone,
And its worth will never be sold.

Scan the QR code to watch and listen to the musical interpretations of these poems on my YouTube channel.

Explore the Visual Journey in Color

Each poem in this book is accompanied by a photograph that reflects its essence. Due to the constraints of the printed format, these images have been published in black and white.

However, if you wish to experience these photographs in their full, vibrant colour, I invite you to scan the QR code below.

This will take you to my Instagram page, where you can explore the images as they were originally intended.

* 9 7 9 8 8 9 5 8 8 0 4 3 2 *